# Handy Kansas Genealogy Handbook

I0450184

## By Gary L. Morris

©2015 Gary L. Morris

ISBN-13: 978-1507530801

ISBN-10: 1507530803

Table of Contents

# Notes

## Genealogical Research in Kansas

Tracing your family history in Kansas can be a fascinating trip through time. Exciting characters such as Wyatt Earp, Buffalo Bill Cody, Wild Bill Hickok, and Bate Masterson color its past. Locating the relevant genealogical records you'll need to find your ancestors however can be a frustrating experience. To help you avoid those frustrations when tracing your Kansas ancestry, we'll show you which records you'll need, and help you to understand:

- What they are
- Where to find them
- How to use them

These records can be found both online and off, so we'll introduce you to online websites, indexes and databases, as well as brick-and-mortar repositories and other institutions that will help with your research in Kansas. So that you will have a more comprehensive understanding of these records, we have provided a brief history of the "Sunflower State" to illustrate what type of records may have been generated during specific time periods. That information will assist you in pinpointing times and locations on which to focus the search for your Kansas ancestors and their records.

## A Brief History of Kansas

Native Americans were the first inhabitants of Kansas; the first Europeans, who were Spanish, explored the area in 1541. Disappointed at finding no treasure, the Spanish returned to Mexico and though the area was frequented by French traders, no country really claimed the area until the United States took control via the Louisiana Purchase in 1803. Between 1812 and 1821, Kansas was considered part of the Missouri Territory, and being on the Santa Fe Trail, was a stop-off point for traders transporting silver and furs from Santa Fe, New Mexico and manufactured goods from Missouri.

The first permanent settlement of white Americans was established at Fort Leavenworth in 1827. The Spanish had claimed the southwest of Kansas, but ceded that area to the United States at the conclusion of the Mexican-American War in 1848. When the Kansas-Nebraska Act was enforced in 1854, Kansas became a separate U.S. Territory. Many settlers from Arkansas and Missouri flocked to the eastern part of Kansas during this time, and as they were from the south, attempted to sway public opinion in favour of slavery.

A second group of settlers however were from Free states such as Massachusetts, and as abolitionists, attempted to end slavery, especially from neighbouring Missouri. Between 1854 and 1861, a number of violent skirmishes took place between the two groups, a preview to the Civil War that was to come. Kansas joined the Union as a slave-free State in 1861, and by that time the violence between pro-slavery factions and abolitionists had pretty much subsided.

At the commencement of the Civil War however, guerrilla raids into Kansas were launched from its borders, and on August 21, 1863, a group of marauders led by William Quantrill, a Confederate bushwhacker, entered Kansas City, killing nearly 200 people and destroying a large part of the city. Though his actions were condemned by the official Confederate military, the damage was already done.

Following the Civil War, many veterans established homesteads in Kansas, and approximately 10,000 African Americans flocked to the area. At the same time, the famous trail established as a cattle drive, the Chisholm Trail, was opened, and the famous frontier towns such as Abilene and Dodge City saw the legends of Wild Bill Hickok and Wyatt Earp born.

**Important Dates in Kansas History**

- **1803** - United States acquires Kansas in the Louisiana Purchase

- **1821** - Santa Fe Trail opened

- **1827-1853** -United States Army builds forts to protect trade along the Santa Fe Trail

- **1830-1854** -Part of Indian Territory - closed to white settlement

- **1838** - "Trail of Death" - Potawatomi Indians removed from Indiana to Kansas

- **1854** - Kansas-Nebraska Act – Kansas becomes separate territory

- **1857** - Battle of Solomon Fork

- **29 January 1861**- Admitted to the Union as a free state.

- **1861-1865** - Civil War

- **1867** -Medicine Lodge Peace Treaty was signed and land south of the Kansas border declared to be Indian territory

- **1872** – Dodge City founded

**Famous Battles Fought in Kansas**

There are two major wars that directly affected the area known as Kansas, the Civil War and the Plains Indian Wars. There was also a skirmish or two that took place on Kansas land during the Mexican-American War. Below you fill find a list of the major battles that took place on Kansas soil along with links to websites where you can learn more about them.

These battle accounts can be very effective in uncovering the military records of your ancestor. They can tell you what regiments fought in which battles, and often include the names and ranks of many officers and enlisted men.

**Love's Defeat, 1847** – Mexican American War

**Love's Defeat:**: http://www.santafetrailresearch.com/research/loves-defeat-01.html

**Battle of Solomon Fork**, **1857** – Plains Indian Wars

**Battle of Solomon Fork**: http://skyways.lib.ks.us/orgs/svha/history/misc/01_Battle%20of%20Solomon%20Fork.pdf

**Lawrence Massacre, 1863** – American Civil War

**Lawrence Massacre, 1863**: http://www.kshs.org/p/kansas-historical-quarterly-quantrill-s-raid-on-lawrence/13185

**Battle of Mine Creek, 1864** – American Civil War

**Battle of Mine Creek**: https://www.kshs.org/kansapedia/battle-of-mine-creek-october-25-1864/18168

**Battle of the Saline River, 1867** – Plains Indian Wars

**Battle of the Saline River**: http://www.legendsofkansas.com/indianbattles.html

**Common Kansas Genealogical Issues and Resources to Overcome Them**

**Boundary Changes**: Boundary changes are a common obstacle when researching Kansas ancestors. You could be searching for an ancestor's record in one county when in fact it is stored in a different one due to historical county boundary changes. The **Atlas of Historical County Boundaries** can help you to overcome that problem. It provides a chronological listing of every boundary change that has occurred in the history of Kansas.

**Atlas of Historical County Boundaries**: http://publications.newberry.org/ahcbp/documents/KS_Consolidated _Chronology.htm#Consolidated_Chronology

**Name Changes**: Surname changes, variations, and misspellings can complicate genealogical research. It is important to check all spelling variations. Soundex, a program that indexes names by sound, is a useful first step, but you can't rely on it completely as some name variations result in different Soundex codes. The surnames could be different, but the first name may be different too. You can also find records filed under initials, middle names, and nicknames as well, so you will need to **get creative with surname variations** and spellings in order to cover all the possibilities. For help with surname variations read our instructional article on **How to Use Soundex**.

**get creative with surname variations**: http://obituarieshelp.org/blog/?p=634

**How to Use Soundex**: http://obituarieshelp.org/blog/?p=505

## Kansas Genealogical Organizations and Archives

Genealogical resources include not only records, but the organizations that house them, or can direct you to them. These institutions include: *Archives, Libraries, Genealogical Societies, Family History Centers, Universities, Churches, and Museums.*

Following are links to their websites, their physical addresses, and a summary of the records you can find there.

Kansas Archives

**Kansas Historical Society** (State Archives) – county records, census, manuscripts, historical newspapers, maps, photographs, Native American index, surname list, military name index

6425 SW 6th Avenue
Topeka, KS 66615-1099
Tel: 785-272-8681

**Kansas Historical Society**: http://www.kshs.org/portal_genealogy

**National Archives at Kansas City** - naturalization records, Native American records, census records, and immigration records

400 West Pershing Road
Kansas City, MO 64108.
Phone: 816-268-8000
E-mail: kansascity.archives@nara.gov

**National Archives at Kansas City**:
http://www.archives.gov/kansas-city/

**Kansas State University** – manuscript collections, literary papers, diaries and journals, photographs, broadsides, maps, audio visual items, oral histories, and printed material.

University Archives
Farrell Library
Manhattan, KS 66506
Tel: (913) 532-7456
E-mail: arcford@ksuvm.ksu.edu

**Kansas State University** link to: http://www.lib.k-state.edu/

## Kansas Genealogical and Historical Societies

Genealogical and historical societies have access to extensive catalogues of genealogical data. They are also able to offer expert guidance for genealogical researchers. Many members are professional genealogists who are most willing to share their expertise in finding ancestors.

**Kansas Genealogical Society** – extensive library holding more than 15,000 books and manuscripts; thousands of vital records, cemetery records and census records

KGS, PO Box 103
Dodge City, KS 67801-0103
Tel: (620) 225 - 1951
Email: kgslibrary@gmail.com

**Kansas Genealogical Society**: http://www.kgs-genlibrary.com/

**Topeka Genealogical Society** – original Probate and Naturalization records, marriage license applications, tax books, cemetery records, city directories, local histories and more

P.O. Box 4048
Topeka, KS 66604-0048
Tel: (785) 233-5762
Email
General Inquiry: webmaster@tgstopeka.org

**Topeka Genealogical Society**: http://www.tgstopeka.org/

**Kansas Heritage Center** – selected Kansas and U.S. census records, military records from Fort Dodge

PO Box 1207
Dodge City KS 67801-1207
Tel: 620-227-1616
Fax: 620-227-1701
E-mail: library@ksheritage.org

**Kansas Heritage Center**:
http://www.ksheritage.org/research_tools.html

## Additional Kansas Genealogical Resources

Kansas Mailing Lists

Mailing lists are internet based facilities that use email to distribute a single message to all who subscribe to it. When information on a particular surname, new records, or any other important genealogy information related to the mailing list topic becomes available, the subscribers are alerted to it. Joining a mailing list is an excellent way to stay up to date on Kansas genealogy research topics. Rootsweb have an extensive listing of **Kansas Mailing Lists** on a variety of topics.

**Kansas Mailing Lists**:
http://lists.rootsweb.ancestry.com/index/usa/KS/misc.html

Kansas Message Boards

A message board is another internet based facility where people can post questions about a specific genealogy topic and have it answered by other genealogists. If you have questions about a surname, record type, or research topic, you can post your question and other researchers and genealogists will help you with the answer. Be sure to check back regularly, as the answers are not emailed to you. The Kansas Message Boards at **Rootsweb** are completely free to use.

**Rootsweb**:
http://boards.rootsweb.com/localities.northam.usa.states/mb.ashx

Kansas Newspapers and Periodicals

Many genealogy periodicals and historical newspapers contain reprinted copies of family genealogies, transcripts of family Bible records, information about local records and archives, census indexes, church records, queries, land records, obituaries, court records, cemetery records, and wills. The following sites have historical Kansas newspapers and periodicals that you can search online or on-site.

**Kansas Historical Society** (State Archives) – African American publications, Civilian Conservation Corps, Labour Populist publications, Socialist publications, Territorial period newspapers, History of Kansas newspapers from1916

6425 SW 6th Avenue
Topeka, KS 66615-1099
Tel: 785-272-8681

**Kansas Historical Society**: http://www.kshs.org/p/kansas-digital-newspaper-program/16126

**Kansas Heritage Center** – most of the newspapers published in Dodge City from 1876 to the present and newspapers from several other Kansas towns.

PO Box 1207
Dodge City KS 67801-1207
Tel: 620-227-1616
Fax: 620-227-1701
E-mail: library@ksheritage.org

**Kansas Heritage Center**:
http://www.ksheritage.org/research_tools.html

**GenealogyBank.com** – free searchable database of Kansas newspaper archives, 1841-1981

**GenealogyBank.com**:
http://www.genealogybank.com/gbnk/newspapers/explore/USA/Kansas/

**Library of Congress Digital Newspaper Directory** – free searchable database of historical U.S. newspapers dating from 1690-present

**Library of Congress Digital Newspaper Directory**:
http://chroniclingamerica.loc.gov/search/titles/

**The Online Books Page** – links to historical books and periodicals available for viewing online, dating from mid-16th century

**The Online Books Page**:
http://onlinebooks.library.upenn.edu/webbin/book//browse?type=lcsubc&key=Kansas%20--%20History%20--%20Periodicals

**NewspaperArchive.com** – largest online database of historical newspapers in the world.

**NewspaperArchive.com**: http://newspaperarchive.com/

## Historical Kansas Maps and Gazetteers

Maps are an integral part of genealogical research. They help us to locate landmarks, towns, cities, parishes, states, provinces, waterways and roads and streets. They also help us to determine when and where boundary changes might have taken place, and give us a visualization of the area we're researching in.

For locating place names, a gazetteer is the best possible resource for any genealogist. Gazetteers are also sometimes called "place name dictionaries", and can help you to locate the area in which you need to conduct research. Below are links to the maps and gazetteers for research in Kansas.

**Peabody GNIS Service – Kansas**:
http://peabody.research.yale.edu/cgi-bin/Query.GNIS?ST=Kansas&SU=1

**Color Landform Atlas – Kansas**:
http://fermi.jhuapl.edu/states/ks_0.html

**1985 U.S. Atlas** : http://www.livgenmi.com/1895/KS/

**Kansas Hometown Locator**: http://kansas.hometownlocator.com/

Kansas City Directories

.

City directories are similar to telephone directories in that they list the residents of a particular area. The difference though is what is important to genealogists, and that is they pre-date telephone directories. You can find an ancestor's information such as their street address, place of employment, occupation, or the name of their spouse. A one-stop-shop for finding city directories in Kansas is the **Kansas Online Historical Directories** which contains a listing of every available historical directory related to Kansas.

**Kansas Online Historical Directories**:
https://sites.google.com/site/onlinedirectorysite/Home/usa/ks

**Kansas Historical Society** (State Archives) – Kansas State Gazetteer and Business Directories for 1878-1912

6425 SW 6th Avenue
Topeka, KS 66615-1099
Tel: 785-272-8681

**Kansas Historical Society**: http://www.kshs.org/portal_genealogy

**Kansas Genealogical Records**

Birth, Death, Marriage and Divorce Records – Also known as vital records, birth, death, and marriage certificates are the most basic, yet most important records attached to your ancestor. The reason for their importance is that they not only place your ancestor in a specific place at a definite time, but potentially connect the individual to other relatives. Below is a list of repositories and websites where you can find Kansas vital records

Kansas began recording official records of births and deaths in 1911. Marriage licenses were required starting in 1867, but not filed at state level until 1913. Copies of vital records after those dates must be requested from the:

**Kansas Office of Vital Statistics**
Charles B. Curtis State Office Building
1000 SW Jackson Street
Suite 120
Topeka, KS 66612-1221
Tel: 785-296-1400.

**Kansas Office of Vital Statistics**:
http://www.kdheks.gov/vital/index.html

**Kansas Genealogical Society** – various historical vital records
KGS, PO Box 103
Dodge City, KS 67801-0103
Tel: (620) 225 - 1951
Email: kgslibrary@gmail.com

**Kansas Genealogical Society**: http://www.kgs-genlibrary.com/

**Kansas Historical Society** (State Archives) – extensive collection of vital records dating from pre-territorial times

6425 SW 6th Avenue
Topeka, KS 66615-1099
Tel: 785-272-8681

**Kansas Historical Society**: http://www.kshs.org/portal_genealogy

Marriage and Divorce Records

Marriages prior to May 1913 were recorded in the district county courts where the marriage took place. Kansas marriage licenses did not include the names of the parents unless the bride or groom was underage. Records can be found at:

The Kansas Historical Society - (State Archives) – has **County Marriage Records** on microfilm, and a state-wide **Kansas Marriage Index, 1854-1861** that can be searched online.

**County Marriage Records**: http://www.kshs.org/p/county-records-on-microfilm/11121

**Kansas Marriage Index, 1854-1861**: http://www.kshs.org/p/kansas-marriage-index/11315

Divorce records from 1861 until July 1951 were recorded in the **Kansas District Courts**.

Copies of official divorce records after July 1951 can be ordered from the **Kansas Office of Vital Statistics**.

**Kansas District Courts**: http://www.kscourts.org/districts/

**Kansas Office of Vital Statistics**:
http://www.kdheks.gov/vital/divorce.html

Census Reports

Census records are among the most important genealogical documents for placing your ancestor in a particular place at a specific time. Like BDM records, they can also lead you to other ancestors, particularly those who were living under the authority of the head of household.

Federal census records for Kansas exist from 1860 through 1940, and can be found in the following repositories:

**National Archives at Kansas City** - census records for all states 1790-1930

400 West Pershing Road
Kansas City, MO 64108.
Phone: 816-268-8000
E-mail: kansascity.archives@nara.gov

**National Archives at Kansas City**:
http://www.archives.gov/kansas-city/

**Kansas Historical Society** (State Archives) – state census records from 1855-1940

6425 SW 6th Avenue
Topeka, KS 66615-1099
Tel: 785-272-8681

**Kansas Historical Society**: http://www.kshs.org/p/kansas-censuses-1855-1930/10961

**Kansas Heritage Center** – selected Kansas and U.S. census records

PO Box 1207
Dodge City KS 67801-1207
Tel: 620-227-1616
Fax: 620-227-1701
E-mail: library@ksheritage.org

**Kansas Heritage Center**:
http://www.ksheritage.org/research_tools.html

**Kansas Genealogical Society** – county census records

KGS, PO Box 103
Dodge City, KS 67801-0103
Tel: (620) 225 - 1951
Email: kgslibrary@gmail.com

**Kansas Genealogical Society**: http://www.kgs-
genlibrary.com/catalogother/kgscatcensus.html

The **Free Census Project** has transcribed many Kansas indexes and
new material is added daily

**Free Census Project**: http://usgwcensus.org/cenfiles/ks.htm

**Access Genealogy** – Kansas census records from 1855-1930

**Access Genealogy**:
http://www.accessgenealogy.com/census/kansas-census-records.htm

**African American Census Schedules Online** – slave schedules, mortality schedules, slave-owners census

**African American Census Schedules Online**: http://www.afrigeneas.com/aacensus/ga/

**Native Americans in Census Records** (US National Archives)

**Native Americans in Census Records**: http://www.archives.gov/research/census/native-americans/

Kansas Church Records

Church and synagogue records are a valuable resource, especially for baptisms, marriages, and burials that took place before 1900. You will need to at least have an idea of your ancestor's religious denomination, and in most cases you will have to visit a brick and mortar establishment to view them.

Most church records are kept by the individual church, although in some denominations, records are placed in a regional archive or maintained at the diocesan level. Local Historical Societies are sometimes the repository for the state's older church records. Below are links archives that maintain church records, as well as a few databases that can be viewed online.

The **Family History Library** contains many church records from a variety of denominations on microfilm.

**Family History Library**:
http://familysearch.org/learn/wiki/en/Family_History_Library

The **Swenson Center** at Augustana College in Illinois has many Kansas Church records from Evangelical, Lutheran, Baptist, and First Covenant Churches from around the state

**Swenson Center**: http://www.augustana.edu/general-information/swenson-center-/genealogy/church-records/kansas---michigan

The Kansas Historical Foundation has filmed the **Leonardville United Methodist Church Records, 1882-1999**, the **St. Joseph Catholic Church Records, 1887-2002,** and the records of the **Third Presbyterian Church (Topeka, Kansas)** dating from the mid-nineteenth century

**Leonardville United Methodist Church Records, 1882-1999**:
http://www.kshs.org/p/leonardville-united-methodist-church-records/13782

**St. Joseph Catholic Church Records, 1887-2002**:
http://www.kshs.org/p/st-joseph-catholic-church-records/13802

**Third Presbyterian Church (Topeka, Kansas)**:
http://www.kshs.org/p/third-presbyterian-church-topeka-kansas/13803

**Central Repositories for Denominational Records**

Most of the records of individual denominations are kept in central repositories. Below is a list of the major congregational archives for Kansas with links to their websites, physical addresses, and contact information.

Baptist

**American Baptist Historical Society**
1106 South Goodman Street
Rochester, NY 14620
Phone: (716) 473-1740
Fax: (716) 473-1740

**American Baptist Historical Society**: http://abhsarchives.org/

<u>Church of Jesus Christ of Latter-day Saints (Mormons)</u>

Early Mormon Church records for Kansas can be found on film located at the LDS Family History Library in Salt Lake City and can be searched via the **Family History Library Catalog**

**Family History Library Catalog**:
https://familysearch.org/eng/Library/FHLC/frameset_fhlc.asp

<u>Disciples of Christ</u>

**Disciples of Christ Historical Society**
1101 19th Avenue South
Nashville, TN 37212
Phone: (615) 327-1444
Fax: (615) 327-1445

**Disciples of Christ Historical Society**:
http://www.discipleshistory.org/

<u>Methodist</u>

**Baker University Library**
606 Eighth Street
Baldwin City, KS 66006
Phone: (913) 594-8414
Fax: (913) 594-6721

**Baker University Library**: http://www.bakeru.edu/library3

**Deets Library Southwestern College**
100 College Street
Winfield, KS 67156
Phone: (316) 221-8225
Fax: (316) 221-2499

**Deets Library Southwestern College**:
http://www.sckans.edu/library/

## Moravian

**The Moravian Archives**
41 West Locust Street
Bethlehem, Pennsylvania 18018
United States of America
Phone: (610) 866-3255
Fax: (610) 866-9210

**The Moravian Archives**: http://www.moravianchurcharchives.org/

## Presbyterian

**Presbyterian Historical Society**
United Presbyterian Church in the U.S.A.
425 Lombard Street
Philadelphia, PA 19147
Phone: (215) 627-1852
Fax: (215) 627-0509

**Presbyterian Historical Society**o: http://www.history.pcusa.org/

## Roman Catholic

**Diocese of Dodge City**
P.O. Box 137
Dodge City, KS 67801
Phone: (620) 227-1500

**Diocese of Dodge City** : http://www.dcdiocese.org/

**Archdiocese of Kansas City in Kansas**
Chancery Office
12615 Parallel Parkway
Kansas City, KS 66109
Phone: (913) 721-1570
Fax: (913) 721-1577

**Archdiocese of Kansas City in Kansas**: http://www.archkck.org/

Kansas Military Records

More than 40 million Americans have participated in some time of war service since America was colonized. The chance of finding your ancestor amongst those records is exceptionally high. Military records can even reveal individuals who never actually served, such as those who registered for the two World Wars but were never called to duty.

Below are a number of links to websites and archives that contain Kansas military records.

**Kansas Historical Society** (State Archives) – primary and secondary source material including muster rolls and lists of free-state forces, Civil War militia rolls, unit histories and rosters, military pensions index, Spanish American War records, WWI and WWII veterans and registrations indexes

6425 SW 6th Avenue
Topeka, KS 66615-1099
Tel: 785-272-8681

**Kansas Historical Society**: http://www.kshs.org/p/military-records-and-sources/11204

**U.S. National Archives** – WWI Draft registration cards, casualties lists, WWI and WWII service records, Korean War records, Vietnam War records, Civil War and Spanish-American War records, and casualties lists.

**U.S. National Archives**:
http://www.archives.gov/research/military/veterans/online.html

**US Department of Veterans Affairs Nationwide Gravesite Locator** – includes information on veterans and their family members buried in veterans and military cemeteries having a government grave marker.

**US Department of Veterans Affairs Nationwide Gravesite Locator**: http://gravelocator.cem.va.gov/

**United States Index to Indian Wars Pension Files, 1892-1926** –
military pension records of soldiers who fought in the Indian Wars
between 1817 and 1898

**United States Index to Indian Wars Pension Files, 1892-1926**:
https://familysearch.org/search/collection/1979427

**United States Registers of Enlistments in the U.S. Army, 1798-
1914** - index of men who enlisted in the United States Army, 1798-
1914.

**United States Registers of Enlistments in the U.S. Army, 1798-
1914**: https://familysearch.org/search/collection/1880762

**United States Mexican War Pension Index, 1887-1926** - index to
Mexican War pension files for service between 1846 and 1848

**United States Mexican War Pension Index, 1887-1926**:
https://familysearch.org/search/collection/1979390

**Civil War Soldiers Service Records** - Service records for both
Union and Confederate soldiers indexed by soldier's name, rank, and
unit.

**Civil War Soldier Service Records**:
http://go.fold3.com/civilwar_records/

## Kansas Cemetery Records

As convenient as it is to search cemetery records online, keep in mind that there are a few disadvantages over visiting a cemetery in person. They are:

- Tombstone information is not always accurately transcribed
- The arrangement of the graves in a cemetery can be crucial as family members are often buried next to each other or in the same grave. This arrangement is not always preserved in the alphabetical indexes that are found online.

With that information in mind, the following websites have databases that can be searched online for Kansas Cemetery records.

**Kansas Tombstone Transcription Project** - death and burial records

**Kansas Tombstone Transcription Project**:
http://usgwtombstones.org/kansas/kansas.html

**African American Cemeteries Online** – African American, slave, and Native American cemetery records

**African American Cemeteries Online**:
http://africanamericancemeteries.com/ar/

**Access Genealogy** – huge database of Kansas cemetery record transcriptions

**Access Genealogy**:
http://www.accessgenealogy.com/cemetery/kansas-cemetery-records.htm

**Find a Grave** – over 100 million grave records can be searched on this site. Search can be conducted by name, location, or cemetery name.

**Find a Grave**: http://www.findagrave.com/

**Interment.net** - A free online database containing approximately 4 million cemetery records from around the world.

**Interment.net**: http://www.interment.net/

**Billion Graves** – as the name implies, you can search a billion records including headstone photos, transcriptions, cemetery records, and grave locations.

**Billion Graves**:
http://billiongraves.com/pages/search/index.php#cemetery

Kansas Obituaries

Obituaries can reveal a wealth about our ancestor and other relatives. You can search our **Kansas Newspaper Obituaries Listings** from hundreds of Kansas newspapers online for free.

**Kansas Newspaper Obituaries Listings**:
http://obituarieshelp.org/kansas_newspaper_obituaries.html

## Kansas Wills and Probate Records

The documents found in a probate packet may include a complete inventory of a person's estate, newspaper entries, witness testimony, a copy of a will, list of debtors and creditors, names of executors or trustees, names of heirs. They can not only tell you about the ancestor you're currently researching, but lead to other ancestors.

Most of these records must be accessed at a county court or clerk's office, but some can be found online as well. You can obtain copies of the original probate records by writing to the county clerk.

Kansas probate records have been recorded by the probate division clerks of the **Kansas District Courts** and include dockets, wills, oaths, inventories, letters, bonds, appraisements, accounts, court orders, claims, and final settlements.

**Kansas District Courts**: http://www.kscourts.org/districts/

## Kansas Immigration and Naturalization Records

The naturalization process generated many types of records, including petitions, declarations of intention, and oaths of allegiance. These records can provide family historians with information such as a person's birth date and place of birth, immigration year, marital status, spouse information, occupation, witnesses' names and addresses, and more.

Most overseas immigrants came to Kansas through east coast ports such as New, and then traveled by railway to Kansas. Earlier immigrants landed at New Orleans and then traveled by steamboats upriver to Kansas. The **U.S. National Archives** has passenger lists or indexes of American ports for 1820 to 1940, as well as immigration and naturalization records for the entire United States. These records can also be accessed at the **National Archives Regional Branch in Kansas City**

**US National Archives**:
http://www.archives.gov/research/immigration/passenger-arrival.html

**National Archives Regional Branch in Kansas City**:
http://www.archives.gov/kansas-city/

Many children were brought to Kansas on what have become known as the "orphan trains." The **National Orphan Train Complex** has preserved stories and artifacts regarding those who arrived in Kansas on these trains between 1854 and 1829.

National Orphan Train Complex
300 Washington Street
P.O. Box 322
Concordia, Kansas 66901
Telephone: 785-243-4471
Email: info@orphantraindepot.org

**National Orphan Train Complex:** http://orphantraindepot.org/

Kansas Native American Records

**Kansas Historical Society** – Native American census reports

**Kansas Historical Society**: http://www.kshs.org/portal_genealogy

**Access Genealogy** – Kansas Native American census records, tribal histories, and much more

**Access Genealogy**: http://www.accessgenealogy.com/native/kansas-indian-tribes.htm

**U.S. National Archives** - information on American Indians who maintained their ties to Federally-recognized Tribes (1830-1970).

**U.S. National Archives**: http://www.archives.gov/research/native-americans/

**Records of the Bureau of Indian Affairs (BIA)**

**Records of the Bureau of Indian Affairs (BIA)**: http://www.archives.gov/research/guide-fed-records/groups/075.html

**American Indians Records Repository** - records dating from the 1700s including trust, education and other historic Indian Affairs records

American Indian Records Repository
Meritex Enterprises
17501 West 98th Street
Lenexa, KS 66219
Phone: 913-888-0601

**American Indians Records Repository**: http://www.doi.gov/ost/records_mgmt/american-indian-records-repository.cfm

# Missing Matriarchs – Resources for Researching Female Kansas Ancestors

Looking for female ancestors requires an adjustment of how we view traditional records sources. A woman's identity was often under that of her husband, and often individual records for them can be difficult to locate. The following resources are effective in locating female ancestors in Kansas where traditional records may not reveal them.

Marriage and Divorce Records

County marriage records began around 1855 while state-wide registration began in 1913. Divorces are recorded in district courts and many county records have been filmed such as:

1. Bourbon County Probate marriage records, 1855-1919 (film 1434854 ff.) at the Bourbon County Courthouse in Fort Scott
2. Jackson County District Court civil dockets and divorce case files, 1858-1919 (film 1650985 ff.) at the Clerk of the District Court, Jackson County Courthouse in Holton.
3. Bureau of Indian Affairs, Pottawatomie Agency register of marriage licenses, 1901-1905 (film 1015900) at the NARA Midwest region in Kansas City, Missouri
4.

Bibliographies

- *Schoolwomen of the Prairies and Plains: Personal Narratives from Iowa, Kansas, and Nebraska, 1860-1920's,* Mary Hurlbut Cordier (University of New Mexico Press, 1997)
- *An Army of Women: Gender and Politics in Gilded Age Kansas,* Michael Goldberg (Johns Hopkins University Press, 1997)
- *"Exodus to Kansas: in Black Women of the Old West,* William Loren Katz (Atheneum Books, 1995, pgs 41-47)
- *Pioneer Women: Voices From the Kansas Frontier,* Joanna L. Stratton (Simon & Schuster, 1983)

## Selected Resources for Kansas Women's History

Argonia and Western Summer Historical Society
Salter House Museum
PO Box 23
510 Main St.
Argonia, KS 67004

Kansas Collection
Kenneth Spencer Research Library
University of Kansas
Bonner Springs, KS 66012

Kansas State Historical Library
6425 SW 6<sup>th</sup> Ave.
Topeka, KS 66615-1099

## Common Kansas Surnames

The following surnames are among the most common in Kansas and are also being currently researched by other genealogists. If you find your surname here, there is a chance that some research has already been performed on your ancestor.

ALBRECHT, ALLEN, AMSBURY, AMSBURY, BAIRD, BAYLESS, BEEDLES, BEAMAN, BELL, BENNETT, BENTLEY, BEST, BOICOURT, BOONE, BOTKIN , BRAKE, BRODEN, BRODDLE, BROWN, BUCKLES, BUNCE, BURGESS, BURNETT, BURSINGER, CARSON, CHINN, CLOGSTON, COLLINS, CONNER, CORBIN, COX, DALTON, DILLEY, EARP, EBBUTT, EISENHOWER, EKENGREN, ERVIN, FISHELL, FISHER, FLORA, FOWLER, FULLER, GALLAWAY, GEORGE, GOFF,GRUBER, HART, HARRINGTON, HAYS, HELMBurton, HEUBLEIN, HICKOK, HILL, HOBBS, HOBSON, HOGGE, HOGUE, HOLLIDAY, HOWELL, HRENCHIR, HUFFAKER, JACKSON, JAMES, JASTER, JONES, JUNOD, KANDT, KANE, KENDALL, KNUTH, LAWRENZ, LEAVENWORTH, LOWE, MCPHERSON, MASTERMAN, McCAIN, McCANN, McCREARY, McCONNELL, METZKER, MONROE, MORISSE, MULKERN, MULLINS, MURDOCK, PAPIN, PARKEN, PARKER, PERKINS, PITSENBERGER, POPPE, POWERS, PRICE, REAGANS, ROCKEY, ROEHRMAN, ROHLOFF, ROOT, ROSE, RUCKER, RUTZ, SEITZ, SEMISCH, SILKS, SIMPSON, SISSOM, SMITH, SPEALMAN, SPENNER, STAVLUND, STEVENS, STEWART, STRAUSS, STROMQUIST, SWARTZ, SWITZER, TAYLOR, THOMAS, THOMPSON, THORNTON, TOBIAS, TROTT, TRUDE, TUCKER, VARNER, VOHS, WALLING, WALTER, WARFORD, WEICK, WIER, WILLIAMS, WILLIS, WILSON, WISE, WRIGHT, YOUNG, YOUNGER, YUNGEBERG, ZAHNLEY

Gary L. Morris worked from 2009 to 2014 as a professional researcher for a major player in the genealogy field. After tracing his family lineage back to 1683, he found that genealogy could be an expensive undertaking. As such, has decided to publish these helpful guides to share the valuable free information he has discovered during his career to help others trace their family lineages as inexpensively as possible. An avid genealogist himself, he hopes you will find this guide factual, thorough, helpful, and most of all, effective in helping you to find your family members.

www.ingramcontent.com/pod-product-compliance
Lightning Source LLC
Chambersburg PA
CBHW061930280526
45787CB00004B/1554